First printing: April 1998

ISBN: 0-89051-229-9
Library of Congress Number: 97-75948

Printed in the United States of America.

AND GOD SAW
THAT IT WAS GOOD

KEN HAM

Master Books

AND GOD SAW
THAT IT WAS GOOD

Introduction

Now, as never before, Christians need to return to the Book of Genesis. In the pages of this devotional, you'll discover the burden of my heart: to reach the lost for Christ by beginning *at the beginning*.

From my native Australia to England and across to these great United States, I hear a crying out for real answers to life's questions and problems. I am convinced that a reliance on the Bible as it is written is the great liberating truth, especially for this generation.

I hope you and your family enjoy this unique format; it is designed to be used by men and women, whether they be parents, grandparents, brothers, sisters, or what have you. If a particular devotion doesn't quite fit you, pass it along.

I have collected some of the more intriguing topics from my daily radio program and assembled them into a devotional.

Everything in it has its origin in Genesis, chapters 1-11. Although some of the devotions speak about contemporary issues, I want you to see that real history, including our present age, is like a mighty tree rooted in the soil of a 3,500-year-old book. The devotions here are humbly written to explain our existence.

> *And God saw every thing that he had made, and,*
> *behold, it was very good* (Gen. 1:31).

Day 1 — In a perfect world

*For, behold, I create new heavens and a new earth
and the former shall not be remembered,
nor come into mind* (Isa. 65:17).

When we read the Bible, we're told that before sin there was no death or bloodshed or struggle or disease. It was a perfect place. Now, this is very hard for us to understand because we live in a world which is suffering the effects of sin and the effects of the curse that were placed upon the world in judgment because of sin.

But you know, I think we can try to understand what a perfect world would be like by reading about the life of the Israelites. The Bible tells us that they wandered in the desert for 40 years, and yet their clothes and shoes didn't wear out, and their feet didn't swell (Deut. 8:4).

I don't know about you, but my clothes and shoes wear out, and my feet swell. You see, we live in a world today where everything is running down, because of man's fall and the subsequent judgment.

But if God sustains something a hundred percent, it's not going to wear out. That would be a different kind of world, wouldn't it? That's what we've got to look forward to in the new heavens and the new earth.

When I look at my garden, I see much beauty in the plants and flowers, and yet I also can observe ugliness in the horrible thorns and thistles that are there also.

How CAN we explain such a world? You know, only Christianity can offer an explanation, and the answer to the problems. No other religion can.

So what is the answer? Well, the answer's in Genesis, of course. God created a perfect world full of beauty, health and joy. However, the first man rebelled against his Creator, and his sin marred the world. Death, disease, and suffering entered this perfect world — but the Creator himself came and paid the penalty for sin, so that one day this world will be restored to its perfect state again.

❦ ❧

Grandparent: You can be a great influence in the life of a child. Your responsibility to that precious little one who sits on your lap is to point him or her to the unspeakable wonder of God's future for His people. Help the joy of your life see that true, everlasting, happiness is *all* ahead for those who repent and believe the gospel.

❧ ☙

Prayer: Father, Thank You for the opportunity to impact my grandchild's life by presenting Your explanation for our world. Thank You, that we can spend time studying your Word and praying together. Your Word is the truth which sets us free. Help me share this comfort with my entire family. Amen.

Day 2 — *"When is your fetus due?"*

Before I formed thee in the belly I knew thee;
and before thou camest forth out of the womb
I sanctified thee (Jer. 1:5).

Years ago, people generally believed that God was Creator, and, therefore, God set the rules. Consequently, abortion was wrong, based upon what the Bible said. However, that foundation in society has been slowly eroded and replaced with another foundation: evolution.

This foundation teaches people that they're just animals in the struggle for survival as life has evolved over millions of years. Therefore, what develops in a woman's womb is only an animal.

It's interesting to note that the increase in the rate of abortion has gone hand in hand with the increasing popularity of evolution.

You see, evolutionists used to believe that when an embryo develops in its mother's womb, it goes through all the evolutionary stages, such as a tadpole, a fish stage (with gill slits!), then it becomes an amphibian, and then on to the reptile stage, and so it goes on.

Now we know that as a human embryo develops, it does go through a stage where it has some pouches, but these pouches are not gill slits or anything like that. In fact, they form into such things as the tonsils, the middle ear canals, and the special glands that form part of our immune system.

The sad part of all of this is that many women thought that when they were aborting their baby, they were actually aborting an animal. This false evolutionary teaching has had disastrous effects on our culture.

A fertilized egg is an individual right from conception, as the Bible teaches. As any biologist should know, the fertilized egg develops in the mother's womb separately from the mother, but relying on the mother's blood supply for nourishment and so on.

When a woman is expecting, we don't say, "When is your fetus due?" Rather, we say, "When is your baby due?"

⁂

Mom: Perhaps you know someone who is facing the heart-wrenching dilemma of a daughter facing an unplanned pregnancy. Maybe the girl's father is angry, or worse, doesn't know. There is often a high cost to doing what is right, but underlying all this is the fact that an innocent baby is alive inside this young woman's womb. Don't be deceived by the lie that abortion is justified by a fraudulent theory, or that the baby is inconvenient. Man says the baby is an animal; the Bible says he or she is made in God's image.

Prayer: Father, I know of a woman in a situation that could tear her family apart. The future is more uncertain than ever. Please give her and her family the grace to bring that precious life into the world. Amen.

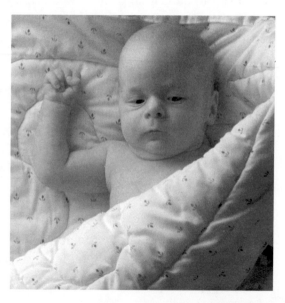

And God Saw That It Was Good

Day 3 — A lot of water and a little bit of time

> *And the waters returned from off the*
> *earth continually: and after the end of*
> *the hundred and fifty days*
> *the waters were abated* (Gen. 8:3).

On a recent airline flight, I picked up a milk carton and noticed that on the outside of it there was a description of how the Grand Canyon supposedly formed. And guess what they said: millions of years of slow erosion by the Colorado River formed the canyon. In other words, a long time and a little bit of water.

For decades, creation scientists have been telling evolutionists that the evidence from the Grand Canyon doesn't fit with this idea of millions of years, and that the canyon had to be gouged out quickly by a large quantity of water. Evolutionists are now conceding this point — they've realized that if the Colorado River did slowly erode the canyon over millions of years, there should be a massive delta where all this sediment would have accumulated.

But no such delta exists. Also, it's now recognized that the processes at the Grand Canyon today are not the same ones that formed the canyon, because the rocks are all covered in a desert varnish.

An event in 1981 brought the evolutionist's theories about the Grand Canyon into question. The traumatic eruption of Mt. St. Helens tore the landscape in Washington state. The devastation included flooding that carved out a canyon 1/40th the size of Grand Canyon. And this smaller canyon was formed in a matter of days! Creation scientists have studied this eruption and its aftermath in trying to understand a post-flood world.

Creationists believe that the aftermath of Noah's flood had a lot to do with the formation of the Grand Canyon.

Can scientists know how the Grand Canyon formed? The answer is in Genesis — a little bit of time and a LOT of water — totally opposite to what the evolutionists tell us.

❧ ☙

Family: A trip to the Grand Canyon is tremendous fun. The sheer size and beauty are literally breathtaking. But realize that even on a tour, and in public information, the origin of this natural wonder is shaded by evolutionary propaganda. Do a little research yourself, and see why true earth history always lines up with the Bible.

⋺⋵

Prayer: Father, this mammoth canyon has been used to turn people toward evolution. May Your light shine into the darkness of this godless theory, and bring people to a right understanding of You, Your judgment, and Your plan of salvation. Amen.

Day 4 — Dinosaurs? In the Bible?

*And God said, Let the earth bring forth the
living creature after his kind, cattle,
and creeping thing, and beast of the earth
after his kind: and it was so* (Gen. 1:24).

Why aren't dinosaurs mentioned in the Bible? I've heard this
question thousands of times.

You might wonder what dinosaurs have to do with quiet time
with God. Let me see if I can answer!

For many years secular science has maintained that dinosaurs
lived long before man. Many Christians become so confused about
the origin of these "terrible lizards" that they try to push the question out of their minds.

I actually believe dinosaurs are mentioned more than many
other animals in the Bible. You see, the word "dinosaur" is not in
the Scriptures because it wasn't invented until the year 1841. Dinosaurs were called dragons before the word "dinosaur" was invented. And the word "dragon" appears in the Old Testament a
number of times.

❧ *And God Saw That It Was Good* ❧

I believe there's even a very detailed description of a dinosaur in the Bible. In Job 40:15 we have a description of an animal called behemoth, which is described as the largest land animal that God made. Now this certainly couldn't refer to an elephant, or a hippopotamus, or anything like this.

Actually, as you read on in this description, it says it had a tail like a cedar tree. Now some Christians have thought that this refers to an elephant. But an elephant's tail looks nothing like a cedar tree. It looks more like a little bit of rope dangling in the wind. If behemoth *was* a dinosaur, that means Job lived alongside dinosaurs, which means that dinosaurs survived the flood on Noah's ark.

These ideas are so radical in our day because we've been literally indoctrinated by evolutionary teaching for generations. It is almost universally accepted that dinosaurs became extinct some 65 million years before man appeared. And yet the Bible tells us that God made the great land animals on Day 6! All of them!

How can we find out about dinosaurs? The answer's in Genesis. God created them, and they lived beside people.

Teen: If you have rejected the Bible because you can't reconcile the tale of the dinosaurs with the Word of God, take heart. God has given us the truth of history in His Word — the Holy Bible. Do some research on your own, but begin with what the Scriptures say, and discover the real story behind these magnificent creatures!

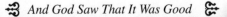

Prayer: Father, in my talks with You, I've wondered about how dinosaurs fit into history. I pray that You will give me strength and discernment to find answers to difficult questions. Amen.

And God Saw That It Was Good

Day 5 — You old fossil!

For this they are willingly ignorant of, that by the word of God the heavens were of old, and the earth standing out of the water and in the water: Whereby the world that then was, being overflowed with water, perished (2 Pet. 3:5-6).

Man's sin marred God's perfect world, and not so long after the Creation week judgment came in the form of a flood. A global catastrophe. And yet, this story is high on the myth list in today's world.

The evidence for this tragedy is so obvious, many people miss it.

Actually, I have found that most people think it takes millions of years to make a fossil. This is because they're so indoctrinated by evolutionary ideas. I have an evolutionist's book that explains to me how fish fossils form, for instance. They have a picture of a fish in a pond, and then the fish dies, and then it sinks to the bottom, and slowly over long periods of time it's covered by mud, and then it turns into a fish fossil.

However, there are billions of fish fossils in the earth and they're beautifully preserved. Many of them indicate the fish hadn't rotted at all. If you observe what happens when a fish dies, for instance (I don't recommend this), if you put some cyanide in your aquarium, you'll notice that the fish usually don't sink, they float. And then, when they start to sink, they're rotting and falling apart. This process would not result in beautifully formed fish fossils like the ones we observe in the earth today. No, these must have been formed quickly, catastrophically.

I like to show people my favorite fossil. It's actually a fossil hat — a petrified hat. A miner left this soft hat in a mine in Australia and when they came back 50 years later, they found it wasn't a soft hat anymore, it was a hard hat — it had petrified! And that certainly didn't take millions of years.

Noah's flood catastrophically buried billions of creatures that turned into fossils.

꘎ ꘎

Family: It's not a popular subject today, but sin is followed by judgment. That can come in the form of parental punishment over a broken window. And it most assuredly came in the form of Noah's flood, when God had had enough of people who didn't love Him. The world tells us the lie that following Jesus is hard, but really, not following Him is the hard part.

֍ ֍

Prayer: Father, when someone I know laughs at the idea of Noah's ark and flood, help me use that as an opportunity to witness about judgment and salvation. Amen.

Day 6 — The first gospel isn't in Matthew

And I will put enmity between thee and
the woman, and between thy seed
and her seed; it shall bruise thy head,
and thou shalt bruise his heel (Gen. 3:15).

After Adam and Eve sinned in the garden, God didn't leave them without hope. He had created them to love them. The audiences I speak to often don't realize that the good news about Jesus Christ was first proclaimed in the Garden of Eden!

In my children's book, *A is for Adam*, there is a picture of Adam and Eve in the Garden of Eden, clothed in lamb's wool. Beside them is a slain lamb.

This picture is based on the passage in Genesis where we're told that because of sin God made coats of skins and clothed Adam and Eve. God killed an animal to provide the first blood sacrifice because of sin.

This is a picture of what was to come in Jesus Christ, the Lamb of God who taketh away the sin of the world. Because of sin, God brought death into the world. Paul later tells us in his first letter to the Corinthians that death entered the world because of Adam's sin.

The only way for man to come back to God was for a perfect man to suffer death and pay the penalty for sin. God sent His only Son to become a man so that He could die and be raised from the dead enabling those who trust in Him to be saved for eternity.

There are professing Christians today who openly question God's fairness in "not making Jesus available to Old Testament people." The implications of this are that Jesus was wrong when he said that He was the only way to God (John 14:6). But we can show them that man knew about the Redeemer, right from the beginning!

The shedding of blood and clothing of Adam and Eve is a picture of the gospel. If Christians don't believe Genesis is literal history — then the gospel message is not to be taken literally either, as this message is presented in Genesis.

❧ ☙

Sunday school teacher: Your job is one of the weightiest around — instructing people about the good news of Jesus Christ. So many don't realize that God moved to calm the fear that Adam and Eve felt when they sinned. This early reference to the gospel can be a powerful witnessing tool, and will open the hearts of those truly seeking the one true God.

※ ※

Prayer: Father, help me to study thoroughly and be prepared to give an answer to anyone who asks why I have hope in Christ. Amen.

Day 7 — The first three days — what was the light?

This then is the message which we have heard of him, and declare unto you, that God is light, and in him is no darkness at all (1 John 1:5).

I've been asked, "If God created everything in six literal days, then how could the first three days of creation have been ordinary days if the sun wasn't created until the fourth day?

First of all, you don't need the sun to have day and night — all you need is light shining on a rotating earth. Now, do we have light on the first three days of creation? The answer is "Yes!"

On the first day, God created light and separated it from the darkness. Because there is evening and morning, it's obvious that the earth is already rotating and the light is shining from one direction.

Actually, God would need to make the property of light so that sources could then give off light.

Now the question people ask is, where did that light come from? To be honest — I don't know. The Bible doesn't tell us. Now this shouldn't be a worry to us, because if God told us everything we wanted to know, we'd have an infinite number of books. And let's face it — we could never read them all.

What God HAS told us is that there was light on Day 1, which must have come from a temporary source. It was replaced by the sun on Day 4. By the way, evolution teaches that the sun existed before the earth — so obviously, one cannot accept evolution as well as the Bible.

I believe that one of the reasons God left the creation of the sun until the fourth day, was because He knew that many cultures over time would want to worship the sun. Remember, God told the Israelites not to worship it as the heathens did. God was showing that He was the source of all power. So the answer is to worship the God of the creation, NOT the creation He made.

❧ ❧

Mom and Dad: In your own home, you are supposed to share the light of Christ with your family. The Bible tells us that darkness hates the light, so when someone challenges your faith in Christ, be ready to give a good answer.

Prayer: Father, I have questions that I feel are legitimate. When I ponder a so-called difficulty in the Bible, give me the perseverance to find an answer. I rejoice in Your answer, because it points me to You. Amen.

Day 8 — The incredible dancing bees

> *For the invisible things of him from the creation of the world are clearly seen, being understood by the things that are made, even his eternal power and Godhead; so that they are without excuse* (Rom. 1:20).

When people ask me for the best evidence for Creation, I tell them that the design of living things we see around us makes it obvious there is a God.

There are countless examples we could use to show that what Paul says in Romans is true — the evidence that God exists is so obvious, that if you don't believe, you are without excuse.

Let's just consider one example, the dancing bees. Bees have one of the most extraordinary means of communication in the insect world. They actually communicate complex information by dancing!

By watching the dance the scout bee performs, the other bees can tell the distance to the food source, and they can also know the direction to fly — whether they should fly towards or away from the sun, or to the left or right of the sun. All this information is relayed by the elements of the dance — whether the bee turns in a circle, does a figure eight, how fast she wiggles her abdomen, and so on.

This dazzling display of these honeybee dancers is truly amazing. When we consider the complicated steps of the dance, and the detailed information conveyed and understood, we certainly don't see the chance randomness of blind evolution.

There are countless examples of God's design in our world. And we must remember that those who are resistant to the idea of God must be wrestling with these questions of superior design, because we know that the Creator has placed a yearning for himself in every person.

The answer's in Genesis — God created! We're certainly without excuse if we don't believe this obvious fact.

⁂ ⁂

Mom: While your children are still young, take a few minutes to take them by the hand and go outside on a sunshiny day. Point out the bees buzzing around your flowers, and give them the information you've just read. Impressions like this stay with little minds, so that when they grow up to be big minds, biblical instruction will stay in place.

Prayer: Father, Your creation is so majestic, help me first to remember and enjoy it. Then, show me opportunities to share this with those I come in contact with. Amen.

And God Saw That It Was Good

Day 9 — *Flying fish — evidence of creation*

*And he saith unto them, Follow me, and I will make
you fishers of men* (Matt. 4:19).

An article was recently published in which a scientist was puzzled as to why flying fish were so colorful. Why was this such a problem to him?

Well, it's only a problem because he's an evolutionist. What evolutionists call problems, really are evidences against their theory.

But let me explain the flying fish. While sailing the tropical seas, this scientist was puzzled about flying fish. Not so much about why they fly, but why they've got such colorful wings.

These flying fish have yellow, brown, and turquoise wings, and shades ranging from frosted purple to deep navy. Now, why is this such a problem to the evolutionists? Well, the wings are only extended during flight, so this is the only time the colors can be seen. What confuses them is this: Why would evolution give these fish beautifully colored wings, which are not used to help them when swimming in the water — to blend into coral colors and so evade capture or anything like that. Why would they have such colors that are only seen when they fly over the water?

Well, the real answer is in Genesis. The flying fish didn't evolve. They are a product of the master designer, the creator God of the Bible, who created everything with a purpose to show forth His power and majesty.

❄ ❄

Dad: When you are on a fishing trip with your son, and your own father, what a wonderful chance exists to discuss God's marvelous designs for fish! The Bible tells us to instruct our children in the ways of God all through the day, in all types of situations. This is an excellent chance to remind two generations of the vastness of God's creative splendor.

❄ ❄

Prayer: Father, the oceans bulge with life. Your presence is so obvious. As I meditate on the diversity of life on this planet, help me share the good news of an indescribably beautiful future in heaven with those I come in contact with. Amen.

❄ *And God Saw That It Was Good* ❄

Day 10 — God's Word, or Star Trek?

The heaven, even the heavens, are the Lord's,
but the earth hath He given to the
children of men (Ps. 115:16).

In the last 50 years, talk of unidentified flying objects, and beings from other planets has dominated discussions from the Pentagon to the porch.

Do I believe in UFOs with little green men flying around out there? No, not at all. In fact, I don't think there's intelligent life in outer space or on other planets.

The evolutionists tell us that because they believe evolution is true, life must have evolved millions of times in the universe. These ideas have captured the imagination of not just the general public, but also large segments of the Church. However, I don't accept this.

You see, the Bible tells us that God made the earth first. The sun, moon, and stars were made for signs and for seasons for the earth. The earth is obviously center stage, on which God made the first man, Adam. And, of course, we know that all human beings who have ever lived are descendants of Adam.

Here's a point we can't forget: only descendants of Adam can be saved because Jesus Christ became a man — Paul calls Him the last Adam, a descendant of Adam — so He could die for Adam and all his descendants. If there were other races of people in outer space, there would be no salvation for them.

Is there life in outer space? The world might say yes, and pursue it with high-tech instruments and research money, but when we start from the Bible we have the correct way of thinking about this subject. The Bible may be silent about animal life and plant life in outer space, but there cannot be a race of biological intelligent beings for the reasons given above.

The next time someone tells you there is life on other planets, ask him or her to provide solid proof. When that doesn't happen, open your Bible and see what the Creator of the universe has to say.

⪧ ⪦

Teacher: It's difficult to resist waves of popular entertainment. Television, film, and books compete for the minds of our families.

But when evolution says there just has to be intelligent life on other planets, it's our duty as Christians to tell the world the truth: that Jesus Christ came to save the people of this unique planet.

❧ ☙

Prayer: Father, discernment is not a sought-after quality these days. Help me have the courage to tell people that there is only one gospel. Amen.

Day 11 — Man's best friend — a biological disaster!

> *They shall perish; but thou remainest;*
> *and they all shall wax old as*
> *doth a garment* (Heb. 1:11).

I've heard dogs called many different names but would you believe a "biological disaster?"

Some time ago, I was telling a veterinarian who attended one of our Answers in Genesis seminars that my wife had just obtained a small dog for our children.

This vet looked at me and said, "Ken, I hope you realize what sort of biological disaster you have there." I asked him what he meant, and he said, "Unfortunately, the dog you have has all sorts of problems; you'll need to make sure it gets its injections, tablets, and have it groomed regularly. Actually, Ken, I make a living out of keeping these biological disasters alive." (I've heard it said that poodles are the perfect example of one of these so-called "biological disasters," but that's another story!)

What he was telling me was that these domestic breeds have all sorts of mutations or mistakes in their genes, and if we let these dogs out in the wild, they would soon die. This vet said that he uses this information to speak against evolution to his customers.

You see, many people think that the fact we see changes in the dog kind is a sort of upward evolutionary change. However, this is certainly not evolution — it's really just variation within the dog kind that God originally made. And the dogs aren't improving; in fact, quite the opposite.

One of the stumbling blocks in the story of Noah's ark is that people wonder how all those animals could have fit. But, you see, we miss the point that Noah took only representatives of *kinds*, not individual breeds (example: Labradors, terriers, and, yes, poodles). In the case of dogs, the one dog kind made the watery journey.

As Dr. Henry Morris has pointed out, these genetic mistakes make it quite clear that the entire universe is winding down, not becoming better and better. The next time you see a dog that is, shall we say, a little less than lovely, remember that this is a prime example of de-evolution, *not* evolution.

Grandpa: When grandchildren come to visit, you are often the "keeper of the pets." Use a fun afternoon at the park with the dog and kids to make a biblical point about the varying kinds that God created during the six days.

Prayer: Father, You have made animals for our happiness. Thank You for the loyal dog curled up at my feet, and for reminding me once again that You alone create and sustain. Amen.

Day 12 — A little good-natured ribbing

*And the Lord God caused a deep sleep to fall
upon Adam and he slept: and he took one of his
ribs, and closed up the flesh instead thereof;
And the rib, which the Lord God had taken
from man, made he a woman* (Gen. 2:21-22).

I've heard a number of people over the years say that men must have one less rib than a woman, because God took a rib from Adam to make Eve. But it is not correct that men have one less rib. Is it?

Let me say loudly: men and women have exactly the same number of ribs. Now it's important to explain this, as I have had a number of people ask me if men have one less rib than a woman because of the account of the creation of Eve in Genesis.

Just because God took a rib from Adam to make Eve would NOT mean that all of Adam's descendants who are males would have one less rib. It is our genes that determine how many ribs a person has.

For instance, if someone had an accident and lost a finger, or even an arm, and then had offspring, the children would NOT have one less finger or one less arm. This is because the blueprint for our body is in the genes, the DNA, in our cells. If you lose something like a rib or an arm, this in no way affects the genes which we pass on to our children.

Secondly, even Adam would have his missing rib back quite quickly, as ribs do regenerate. I know many sincere Christians who back themselves into a corner by insisting that Genesis can be supported by the medical fact that men have one less rib than women. You see the error of this thinking!

And this is the important point: multitudes of people reject God's word because of alleged discrepancies, or outright contradictions. I challenge you to increase your faith by really studying to see that it is not the Bible that is in error, but man's perceptions!

᧥ ᧤

Wife: The reality of the woman coming into existence after God took a rib from the man underscores the intimacy you share in your marriage. God instituted the family unit, and you are to stick with your husband as one flesh, in order to nurture a healthy family. There is no greater calling.

⚜ ⚜

Prayer: Father, help me and my spouse to see that this kindness from God made it possible for us to experience true intimacy in marriage. I thank God for the person You gave me. Amen.

Day 13 — Humans and animals — similar or separate?

All flesh is not the same flesh: but there is one kind of flesh of men, another flesh of beasts, another of fishes, and another of birds (1 Cor. 15:39).

In a recent magazine article, it was written that "no single essential difference separates human beings from other animals."

I get so frustrated when I read these ridiculous statements. Are we just like the animals? If people just thought about this for a moment, they would realize how wrong this kind of thinking is. Is there really no single, essential difference that separates humans from other animals? Let's put tongue in cheek and consider the following:

Apes, like humans, have well-formed rational abilities. Their ability to develop an argument, follow a line of logic, and draw conclusions, is quite remarkable.

Also, like humans, apes have a marked faculty for language — their vocabulary is enormous, their grammar complex, their conversations deep and meaningful.

Like humans, apes also have a strong spirit of inquiry. Their research in the fields of astronomy, mathematics, medicine, and physics is particularly noteworthy.

Apes also yearn for meaning in life. This is why they devote so much of their time to philosophy, theology, and ethics. Their creative impulse, like humans, is seen in their poetry, painting, dance, drama, and music.

We could go on and on. The point is, there is a great gap between apes and humans. Apes are animals. However, the answers from Genesis tell us that man is not an animal, man is made in the image of our Creator.

And yet, secular science weaves elaborate tales of human evolution, and men and women accept it without question. But this is a fairly recent phenomena, arising from 19th century attacks on the infallibility of Scripture.

Even among theologians, there are vast numbers of people who believe God used a cruel, violent method like evolution, rather than create as He plainly revealed in Genesis. Man isn't getting better, he's just inventing new ways to dishonor God.

＃ ℰ

Pastor: You have been entrusted with the spiritual health of your congregation. More than likely, you have been taught to downplay those portions of the Bible that are labeled "divisive," such as special creation. Remember that this mindset eliminates most of the Bible! In the privacy of your office, take a few moments to reflect on the simplicity of the biblical revelation. Let it bless you and your flock.

＃ ℰ

Prayer: Father, help my own unbelief or bias, let me be conformed to your image and your will. If I have missed a key piece of Your Word, let that illuminate my heart, so that I in turn can share with Your people. Amen.

Day 14 — Jet propulsion — who invented it?

And God said, Let the waters bring
forth abundantly the moving creature
that hath life (Gen. 1:10).

It is commonly believed that jet propulsion is a modern invention. However, it actually goes way back — in fact to the beginning of Creation.

That's right — jet propulsion isn't so modern after all! It was in use 6,000 years ago. Not in a jet airplane, but in a class of mollusks known as cephalopods.

Most people will be familiar with the squid, a fascinating creature that can travel at 34 miles per hour by squirting a strong jet of water from a tube or funnel. Muscles contract to force a narrow jet of water through the funnel, and the squid rockets off — backwards. Then, turning the funnel 180 degrees, it can go forward. Surely, an honest person couldn't believe in the randomness and waste of evolution after considering the engineering feats of a squid.

You know, we often stand in awe when we watch a jumbo jet

with its large engines. As we watch this man-made machine, we give praise and honor to the inventors who designed the complex jet engines and the aircraft.

But, how often do we reflect on the fact that what man has done in reality is to copy the original invention? You see, God invented flying machines like birds in the first place. He also invented jet propulsion in creatures such as the squid. We simply are discovering these things on our own for the first time.

Take a moment to analyze the praise given to men like Edison, Orville and Wilbur Wright, and others. I wonder how many of history's great inventors gazed out at sea, or shielded their eyes to watch the miracle of flight in birds . . . and gave pause to marvel at God's creative powers.

If we give such praise and honor to the human designers, how much more should we give praise and honor to the original designer — the Lord Jesus Christ.

꿈 꿈

If you are a science instructor, what a marvelous opportunity you have to bring about good! The wonders of creation provide a limitless supply of lessons and study for those entrusted to you in the classroom. Take a few minutes today to describe the inventor of jet propulsion!

⁂ ⁂

Prayer: Father, Your awesome diversity overwhelms me and humbles me. Every day, new discoveries of science reveal creatures we couldn't imagine on our own. Give me the knowledge and desire to make this plain to others. Amen.

Day 15 — Environmental issues
— they're for Christians, too

And God blessed them, and God said unto them,
Be fruitful, and multiply, and replenish the earth,
and subdue it: and have dominion over the fish of the sea,
and over the fowl of the air, and over every living
thing that moveth upon the earth (Gen. 1:28).

Environmental concerns and issues are continually in the news, it seems. Usually, it's the evolutionists who get very vocal about these matters, and in fact, Christians are often accused of destroying the environment. Should Christians be involved in environmental issues?

I believe that yes, Christians should lead the way in such matters, as they should have a true understanding of this world and its purpose and meaning.

But, sadly, it's mainly people who reject God's Word who are active in environmental matters, and they have the wrong motives and reasoning.

For instance, you will hear environmentalists get very vocal about saving whales, and yet at the same time they will often defend abortion, which results in killing millions of human beings. They may stop timber harvesting in an area because of a particular animal, yet they are happy to try to destroy the AIDS virus. Actually, from an evolutionist's perspective — to be truly consistent, they would have to admit that anything that happens must be allowed, as this is a part of evolution.

However, Christians who get their answers from Genesis understand that man is to have dominion over the earth, and that sin has affected the world. Thus, more than ever, man needs to look after God's world, using it for his good and God's glory, not exploiting it for greed. And Christians must understand that we can actively do things to help overcome the effects of the curse.

Remember that there is nothing inherently wrong with litter pickup, or tree planting, or even saving endangered animals. We are to show compassion and let Christ be our example. But the apostle Paul once said that there were people who worship the creation more than the Creator, and that is a very dangerous place to be, indeed.

Day 16 — Equals

all the tribes and nations today are descended from Adam and Eve through Noah and his three sons, Ham, Shem, and Japheth. The event of the Tower of Babel split up the population and spread it over the earth.

It's a shocking and sad fact of history that evolution taught and still does, if we're really honest, that certain cultures are closer to the apes than others. It wasn't that long ago that the Australian Aborigines were thought to be the "missing link" between apes and humans.

By the way, most people don't realize that ALL human beings are in reality exactly the same skin color. We have a pigment called melanin. If you have a lot of melanin, you can be very dark, even black. If you have a little bit of melanin, you can be very light, or you can be any shade in between.

It can be shown quite simply from genetics that if we started with Adam and Eve as middle brown, which is the majority of the world's population, then from these two people, you could have children who are black or light brown, or anywhere in between, in just ONE generation.

❧ ☙

❧ *And God Saw That It Was Good* ☙

Dad: Your children are looking to you for a reaction to people of different skin tones. The Bible tells us that we are not to have malice or hatred in our hearts toward each other. God's Word is very clear that He is saving people out of every nation and tribe . . . He is not excluding people from His kingdom because of the shade of their skin. We are to love our neighbors as ourselves (Matt. 22:39).

Prayer: Father, help me have the courage to tell my child(ren) that God wants us to love all people, no matter what shade of color their skin is. Help me see this for myself, and to share this truth with my family and friends. Amen.

Day 17 — Darwin's house disproves evolution!

Noah's flood was a global catastrophe that formed fossil layers around the world. Darwin was convinced that natural processes had shaped the earth over millions of years.

As a result, Darwin himself said: "I had gradually come by this time to see that the Old Testament was no more to be trusted than the sacred books of the Hindus." This man, who influenced so many, started down the slippery slope of unbelief because he chose not to believe Genesis. Let his destiny be a warning.

⸙ ⸙

Husband: If you are frustrated that your home is "decaying," that it isn't a place of comfort for you and your family, try opening the pages of your Bible and seeing that the only true hope for a house that lasts is trusting God. Lead your family in a Bible study and stick with it.

⸙ ⸙

Prayer: Father, the example of Charles Darwin's home is a powerful reminder that a foundation built on Satan's lies corrupts absolutely. Help us to take God at His word. Amen.

⸙ *And God Saw That It Was Good* ⸙

Day 18 — Sandy beaches . . .
in only a few months?

Fear ye not me? saith the Lord: will ye not tremble at my presence, which have placed the sand for the bound of the sea by a perpetual decree, that it cannot pass it: and though the waves thereof toss themselves, yet can they not prevail; though they roar, yet can they not pass over it? (Jer. 5:22).

Creationists maintain that Noah's flood occurred around 4,500 years ago. But surely there has not been enough time since then to form the sandy beaches we see around the world. Right?

Actually, there's been *more* than enough time. Because of evolutionary indoctrination we've all received, we look at the waves breaking on a beach and think that it must've taken millions of years for the sand and the rock platform to form. However, consider this:

In 1963 in the North Atlantic, a huge undersea volcanic eruption off Iceland formed a new island called Surtsey. An official Icelandic geologist was amazed at what he saw happen on Surtsey.

Day 19 — The missing link is really missing

They were driven forth from among men. . . . To dwell in the clifts of the valleys, in caves of the earth, and in the rocks. (Job 30:5-6).

If you received a public school education, you've probably heard that the so-called "Nebraska Man" was once called a missing link. The discovery was announced far and wide earlier this century. Please allow me to share some fascinating information with you.

The name given to Nebraska Man was *Hesperopithicus Haroldcooki*. Sounds scientific, doesn't it? It is actually the name given to a supposed "ape man" made up on the basis of ONE TOOTH discovered on a farm in western Nebraska by a man named Harold Cook.

He sent the tooth to the Museum of Natural History in New York and told the museum this was from an ape man. Later the *Illustrated London News* ran a story in 1927 about Nebraska Man, even including a picture of this supposed "ape man" AND his wife!

Even the media at the time of the Scopes trial promoted Nebraska Man as the latest evidence that man evolved.

Eventually, it was determined that even this tooth did NOT come from an ape-man, BUT from an extinct pig. Later on scientists found that the pig wasn't even extinct!

So, Nebraska Man was not an ape-man at all. No evidence has ever been found, or ever will be found, to contradict the answer given in Genesis that God created the first man directly from the dust of the ground.

There is a whole list of supposed missing links that have been paraded in front of the public for over a hundred years. Should you ever have the time, contact us at Answers in Genesis (the address is in the back of this book), and we'll be happy to point you toward great resource materials.

The next time you hear about some supposed "ape-man," or "missing link" find, remember Nebraska Man — the pig that made a monkey out of evolutionary scientists!

☙ ❧

Day 20 — Digging for the truth

turned the wombat's pouch around!

Any logical thinking person would ask the question, "Well what happened to the young in the pouch while the pouch was still in the process of turning around?"

What is even more remarkable is that when a marsupial is born it is only the size of a jelly bean, with no eyes or back legs. This little creature knows where to go and how to get into its mothers pouch. It knows what to do when it gets into the pouch and how to get the milk necessary for the rest of its development. As I often say to my children when I look at marsupials like the wombat, "They're designed to do what they do, and what they do, they do very well. Don't they?" My children think they do. They certainly are a marvelous evidence of God's creative power.

This is the answer we have from Genesis — God created everything with plan and purpose.

〜 〜

Teacher: Here we have another example of proof from nature that evolution is preposterous. Point this out on field trips, and let students know the planet is teeming with creatures designed to function the same way they operate today. Something as common as the Australian wombat can be used to build a firm foundation for your student's spiritual development.

❧ ☙

Prayer: Father, You've shown me that the wombat has a job to do as it digs in the earth. Help me to dig for the truth and be as tenacious as the wombat. Amen.

Day 21 — A most terrible enemy

has violated a home close to you, reflect on today's devotion. Resolve to teach young people that they have both a purpose in this life, and an eternal destiny.

☙ ❧

Prayer: Father, this dark curtain has been pulled over many families! Your word says that death is not an enemy; I know that. Please give me the words to say, or the action to take, in order to bring some hope to this situation. Amen.

Day 22 — *The formation of snowflakes*
— is that evolution?

*Hast thou entered into the treasures
of the snow?* (Job 38:22).

Have you ever tramped through a field of fresh snow and meditated on its beauty? As a native of Australia, I haven't done this often, but I'm learning!

We once ran a story in *Creation* magazine, about the beautiful design of the snowflake and how evolutionists like to use it to show how complex life could arise from disorder. How do we answer this one? There's actually no parallel between these two at all. You see, to put it simply, water forming into snowflakes is really doing what comes naturally in freezing conditions. In other words, the properties of water — and the information that's already there in the molecule — cause snowflakes to form under the right conditions. And, when these snowflakes melt, they turn back to water. Then, under the right conditions, the water can again turn into snowflakes.

No two snowflakes are alike. When you think of the countless

Day 23 — Divorce is not of God

And he answered and said unto them,
Have ye not read, that he which made
them at the beginning made them
male and female (Matt. 19:4).

Have you wondered why there are so many breakups of marriages and divorces these days, even within the Church? I have seen this tragedy too many times in my travels.

There are many explanations, but I think there are two major reasons that many people don't even consider.

First of all, people don't understand what it means that God is Creator, and therefore He sets the rules. It's not a matter of our opinions of how we should act in this world — it's a matter of what God says. To understand this, we need to go to His Word.

Now here is the second major reason most people don't understand, and even most Christians don't understand. Marriage is founded in the Book of Genesis. If we want to understand the roles of man and woman, we have to go back to Genesis and be prepared to accept the roles God has ordained for us regardless of our opinions. You see, even Jesus Christ, the Son of God, when asked about divorce, immediately went back to Genesis to explain the foundation of marriage.

The Bible teaches us that the family is the first and most fundamental human institution which God ordained in Scripture. He made the first family when he made the first woman and the first man, Adam and Eve — the first marriage.

Satan, of course, knows that if you destroy the family, you also greatly weaken the backbone of the nation because you destroy that educational unit that God uses to communicate His truths generation after generation. No wonder the family is so much under attack today.

It grieves me to see so many families break up, and I believe the primary reason is, we've gotten away from building our families on the foundation of the Holy Scriptures. Psalm 11:3 says, "If the foundations be destroyed, what can the righteous do?"

❧ ☙

Mom and Dad: Perhaps you know someone who is contemplating divorce. You could be the one to tell that person: *God's promises are sure, for if they are not, we have no hope at all.* Therefore, ask Him to begin healing that marriage, so that that family will grow strong by being built upon God's Word — which is the only way it will last.

Prayer: Father, many marriages have become painful and frustrating. All we can do right now is ask You to heal them. We ask you to turn their hearts to You to heal those marriages. We know divorce is from the evil one. Please give such people renewed hearts and renewed courage to resolve their differences. Amen.

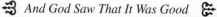

Day 24 — Misplaced anger?

*For God so loved the world, that he gave his
only begotten Son, that whosoever believeth
in him should not perish, but have
everlasting life* (John 3:16).

Death and suffering . . . where did they come from?

Just recently I was in Northern Ireland. I was speaking with a couple whose parents had been blown up by a terrorist bomb. They were very angry with God because of what had happened, and they were blaming God, in fact!

As I spoke to them, I tried to explain that the reason for death and suffering in the world is because of sin. They shouldn't be blaming God. They should be looking at their sin and blaming their sin of rebellion, our sin of rebellion in Adam for the entrance of death and suffering into the world.

You see, it's interesting, the issue of death and suffering is one that comes up in non-Christian and Christian circles alike. But it's only the Christian who believes in a literal Genesis, who understands the origin of death and suffering, who can give the answer as to why there's death and suffering in the world. The Bible tells us that the first man, Adam, brought sin into the world, and death, as the result of sin, as a judgment for his rebellion against the Holy God.

Sadly, the whole question of suffering and death is most often muddled in churches. Scores of pastors either can't articulate the origin of death, or they purposely introduce doubt about Genesis. This leaves their flocks wandering aimlessly, and sometimes some of them get angry at God, who has given them life over death.

As a result of unbelief or indifference, those coping with death and poor health fail to see the answer can only be found in the pages of the Bible.

Why is there death and suffering in the world? The answer's in Genesis. It's because of our sin. Don't blame God! We need to blame our sin.

꒛ ꒜

Family: Perhaps death has hit very close to you. You are angry at God and wondering why He would take this one away. But if we are honest, and sincerely study the Scriptures, we'll see that God is not the enemy. Willful sin brought suffering and death into the world. This can be the start of your healing process.

⦊ ⦉

Prayer: Father, forgive me for blaming this death on You. I know that suffering is an intrusion upon this earth because of sin, and yet You watch over us, as You did Job and others through the centuries. Help me see Your goodness in the world today. Amen.

Day 25 — It does matter

For in six days the Lord made heaven and earth,
the sea, and all that in them is, and rested
the seventh day: wherefore the Lord blessed the
sabbath day, and hallowed it (Exod. 20:11).

Ah, now to my favorite subject.

For over a hundred years, Christians have said that God could have created in six days, or six seconds, or six billion years , and that it doesn't really matter. Can we know for sure?

But, you see, it's not a matter of how long it could've taken God to create — it's how long he said he DID take that is important.

The evolutionists believe that the world is billions of years old, and there are many Christians who think maybe God took billions of years to make the world. Since just before Darwin, it has been very fashionable to first question the biblical account of creation, then openly ridicule it. When a man by the name of Charles Lyell popularized the belief that the earth's rock layers were millions of years old, the idea caught on with shocking speed.

However, the Bible tells us that God is infinite in power. He could make anything at all in NO time.

Actually, the only way you would know how long He took to make the world was if He told us . . . and He did! In God's Word, the Bible, we're told that He took six days to create, and He rested for one day. He did this as a pattern for us — our seven-day week!

If God created everything in 6 billion years — we would have a fascinating week, wouldn't we? None of us would even live through the first day!!

By the way, it might interest you to know that in the past 200 years, totalitarian regimes in France and Russia have tried to force the public to adopt a different number of days in their work weeks. The people couldn't cope, and the six-day work week was re-instituted!

This all gets back to an authority issue: are we going to take God at His Word, or are we going to trust the fallible opinions of fallible, sinful humans?

⁂

Pastor: In the course of a year, you might never mention the literalness of the creation week. If so, you are not alone. But I challenge you to research this issue for yourself. Then, see if the topic doesn't have an impact on your congregation.

Prayer: Father, Your word is truth. I don't want to fall for the oldest lie and question whether You really meant what You said. Help me to rely on the strength of Your Word to me and mankind. Amen.

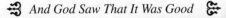

Day 26 — Children are a blessing from the Lord

Train up a child in the way he should go: and when he is old, he will not depart from it (Prov. 22:6).

Surely it's important to teach Bible stories to children. I praise the Lord for all the Bible stories I was taught as a child.

We need to teach our children God's Word from beginning to end. My wife and I spend hours teaching our children to understand the Word of God.

However, we need to do much more than just teach Bible stories.

Most Sunday school curriculums used by Sunday school teachers today basically teach children Bible *stories* such as Jonah and the whale; Jesus on the Cross; Paul's missionary journeys, and so on.

Now these are important, BUT what many teachers haven't realized is that the children today are being bombarded through the media and education system with evolutionary ideas. They come to church and learn Bible stories, but the world is telling them that scientists have proved the Bible is not true, that man evolved from apes, that Noah's ark and flood are just myths.

It is very difficult to get people interested in accounts that have no basis in reality. There is a dominant mindset today that where the ancient past is dealt with biblically, the stories are just that — stories.

What I am saying is that as well as Bible stories, we need to also be teaching children against evolution, and teaching them how they can logically defend creation and the flood and so on. If we don't do this — many of them will reject the Bible stories we taught them.

Myth isn't of much help when death approaches, or relationship problems arise. But the revealed truth of history, as outlined in the Bible, is vital to a hurting world.

❧ ☙

Sunday school director: If you've noticed a general lack of enthusiasm in your classes, take a moment to analyze why that is. If it appears that children as well as adults are bored or confused, could it be that they have been taught Bible stories so long, they no longer consider them real? Learn to teach biblical absolutes that absolutely happened.

⚜ ⚜

Prayer: Father, our church needs an overhaul in our teaching departments — Sunday school, Bible study, etc. Help us to present the truth of Your Word as literal history, so that people will have an anchor for life's decisions. Amen.

Day 27 — A veggie tale

And to every beast of the earth, and to every fowl of the air,
and to every thing that creepeth upon the earth,
wherein there is life, I have given every green herb
for meat: and it was so (Gen. 1:30).

In Genesis 1:30, we're told that God created a perfect world and instructed the beasts of the earth and the fowl of the air and everything that creeps upon the earth to eat every green herb for food. In other words, the animals were created to be vegetarian.

This fits with the fact that the Bible also teaches us that there was no death or bloodshed until after Adam sinned. It also fits with the fact that one day there will be a new heaven and a new earth in which righteousness dwells, where there will be no more death or bloodshed, and the animals will be vegetarian — as they were originally!

In Isaiah, we get a glimpse of this where we're told that in the future the lion, wolf, and lamb will all live together, and the lion will eat straw like an ox. Man was also created to be vegetarian, but was told he could eat meat AFTER the flood.

And God Saw That It Was Good

Once we have our answers from Genesis, we can understand why the world is full of death and suffering — because of sin. The fact that many creatures are not vegetarian today is a continual reminder of man's rebellion against God and his need for a Saviour.

The evolutionist will counter this assertion by saying that if God created and saw that it was good, how do we explain fangs and claws in nature? Again, my answer is that man's sin brought a curse upon the ground and everything that crawled upon it. Thorns grew up. The garden was gone.

By the way, you might be interested to know that there are many creatures today with awful-looking teeth, but they are strictly vegetarian! For instance, most bears are primarily vegetarian, and yet the structure of their teeth is very similar to that of a tiger. In other words, just because an animal has sharp teeth doesn't mean it is a meat-eater, it just means that it has sharp teeth. These sharp teeth can function for eating various plants as well. The male camel looks like a savage meat-eater, and yet it is strictly vegetarian.

꩜　꩜

Dad: If you teach a Sunday school class, use this information to explain the effects of sin on our world. Because people don't read their Bibles, they are easy prey for those who question the paradox of a perfect creation and our present situation. Send your class back to Genesis.

≈ ≈

Prayer: Father, I don't live around wild animals, but I am aware of one who walks about, seeking whom he may devour. Help us to do as the Book of James tells us: "Resist the devil, and he will flee from you" (James 4:7). Amen.

≈ *And God Saw That It Was Good* ≈

Day 28 — Penguin mania

*And God saw every thing that he
had made, and, behold, it was
very good* (Gen. 1:31).

In my work I see many people get excited over dinosaurs. But I'm here to tell you, even penguins declare the brilliant handiwork of the Creator.

Bulletin: scientists at Berlin Technical University have become obsessed with penguins. We reported on this in *Creation* magazine.

As one of the researchers stated, "Everything about the penguin is perfect." This scientist went on to explain that the penguin's body is a natural torpedo, and so is economical on fuel. He believes that penguins are actually more effective models to copy than dolphins or fish.

In fact, a German company is considering producing airships modeled on the penguin's barrel-like body, which it believes will use 30 percent less fuel than the older designs. And now a Japanese firm is designing underwater tankers that look like steel birds!

The penguin researcher went on to say that cars, trucks, and trains will eventually follow. He stated, "We just can't ignore the perfection of the penguins."

The sad thing is that the majority of scientists will acknowledge the beautifully designed penguin, and copy the design features, but then say that all this arose by chance! As we read in Romans, they worship the creature instead of the Creator. I wish scientists would admit that they have to copy what has already been designed — and they can't improve on it.

And what do I say? Well, the answer's in Genesis — God makes a good product, doesn't he? So let's worship the Creator!

꒐ ꒑

Grandpa: If you take your little ones to the zoo, tell them about the amazing design features of our friend, the penguin. Then tell them how aircraft and ships are modeled on these funny creatures. Let them see for themselves that when God makes something, it doesn't need improving.

꒐ *And God Saw That It Was Good* ꒑

※ ❧

Prayer: Father, as I see all these examples of Your perfect design, help me share these tidbits with those who don't know Your Son. Help me see that what some might view as silly — a penguin — could actually draw someone close to You. Amen.

Day 29 — Evolution is swamped again

And the waters prevailed exceedingly
upon the earth; and all the high hills,
that were under the whole heaven,
were covered (Gen. 7:19).

When I went to school, I was told that it took millions of years for plants in a swamp to turn into coal. But is this true?

Scientists have now found that they can make high-grade, black coal in a laboratory in only about 28 days. The process doesn't take millions of years of heat and pressure. In fact, they found that you can convert brown coal into black coal quite easily by using heat and clay.

Not only this, but most of our coal deposits aren't made up from swamp plants. I remember being in Australia at one of the big coal deposits in Victoria and asking the geologist how the coal arrived there.

He said it was a result of plants that grew in swamps over millions of years. I then said to him, "But most of the trees in this coal here have been identified."

And God Saw That It Was Good

"That's right," he said.

"But they've been identified as pine trees," I said.

"That's true," he said.

"But," I said, "those pine trees don't grow in swamps."

"No," he said, "That's a little bit of a problem, but maybe they did grow in swamps millions of years ago."

He didn't want to admit the fact that the evidence didn't fit his theory.

How did coal form? The answer's in Genesis. The water from Noah's flood deposited large quantities of plants all over the world that have become today's coal deposits.

It's ironic, isn't it, that this is another example of God's love and planning, to provide us with heat and energy sources. But though we take advantage of this "benefit" from long-ago judgment, God is still thought of as a myth by much of the world!

Dad: The next time you change the oil in your car, let your sons watch. As you explain the importance of engine lubricants, tell your precious children about God's provision of energy sources, and where oil and coal came from. Your children will begin to see the world through the window of the Bible. In this routine maintenance act, you might plant the seed of salvation.

❧ ☙

Prayer: Father, we are amazed at the wonders of Your creation. Even though we live in a fallen world which has been judged by the flood You sent in Noah's day, we still can see Your mercy displayed throughout our lives and the lives of others. Help us to remember that You are God, and that You judge sin. Yet, You show mercy to all those who trust in You for salvation. Help us also to remember that You make the sun to rise "on the evil and on the good," and you send rain on "the just and the unjust" (Matt. 5:45). Amen.

Day 30 — Just read God's Word!

*It is he that sitteth upon the circle
of the earth* (Isa. 40:22).

A common argument among non-Christians is that in order to take the Bible literally we must believe in a flat earth. Of course, when you read the Bible, you find exactly the opposite situation.

This is another example of evolutionist propaganda designed to make creationists look foolish. One simply needs to look at Scripture to determine if the Bible teaches a flat earth. Sadly, even many Christians fail to look in their Bibles.

In Proverbs, we read that God "set a compass upon the face of the deep." The word compass can mean circle or sphere. In Isaiah we're told that God "sitteth upon the circle of the earth." Again, the reference to the earth is in the context of it being spherical. It couldn't be more plain.

In the Book of Job, we read that God "stretcheth out the north over the empty place, and hangeth the earth upon nothing." The word "nothing" really means "nothing whatsoever." From these verses, we get the idea that the earth is a sphere — that it is suspended in space. This is precisely what we observe when looking at the earth from the space shuttle.

So where did people ever get the idea that the Bible teaches a flat earth? Well, usually they quote the verses from Isaiah and Revelation that talk about the four corners of the earth. But this phrase actually means four *quarters* — which means the division of geography into four quadrants. Direction has nothing to do with the shape of our planet, so don't let scoffers attempt to discredit the Bible.

The Psalmist told us long ago that God's Word is true from the beginning. This reminds me of the warning in 2 Peter 3:3-10 where Peter tells us in the last days scoffers will mock those who believe in God's Word concerning the creation, the flood, and the coming judgment by fire. We need to be bold and proclaim to the scoffers what the Psalmist told us in God's Word that God would intrude upon the beginning.

⁂

Mom: No doubt your family enjoys a home-cooked breakfast. When you're in the kitchen preparing this delicious meal, gather everyone around and have a quick Bible lesson as you prepare biscuits. Roll the flour into a ball, then flatten it. Compare this to the flat-earth theory, then to the Word of God. There are always opportunities to honor God.

❧ ❧

Prayer: Father, Your word is very clear, and available to anyone who seeks truth. If I get the chance, prepare me to answer correctly when people ridicule Your revelation. Amen.

Also by Ken Ham:

A Is for Adam
The Answers Book
D Is for Dinosaur
Genesis and the Decay of the Nations
Jesus Is Calling
Jesus the Child
The Lie: Evolution
The Relevance of Creation
What Really Happened to the Dinosaurs?

Video series:

Answers in Genesis
The Genesis Foundation

and

3-D Dinosaur Cards

Available at bookstores nationwide or write
Master Books, Inc., P.O. Box 727, Green Forest, AR 72638